Random Haikus & Poems

Quentin Renault

BookLeaf Publishing

India | USA | UK

Presentation by *BookLeaf Publishing*

Web: www.bookleafpub.com

E-mail: info@bookleafpub.com

ISBN: 9789358737905

First edition 2023

To Tam,

ACKNOWLEDGEMENT

To all the beautiful disasters and captivating calamities that have graced the pages of my life, I offer my gratitude. You've fuelled my creative fire and given me stories to tell, even when no one wants to hear them.
 You're the muses I never knew I needed.

 To myself, for somehow turning my incoherent ramblings into something resembling literature, you're a damn magician.

 And to all those who've walked the dark and twisted path alongside me, here's to you - may you find your own story in these pages.

PREFACE

Random Haikus & Poems, by Sneaking Wisdom.

Sneaking Wisdom is using social media to... well... sneak wisdom into people's lives.
This book is an amalgam of some poems and haikus I've written along the years, trying to make sense of life, love, friendship, meaning, and more.

Look - Let's be honest, that won't be the best book you've ever read, but who knows ? You might get an idea or two from it !

Instagram : @sneaking.wisdom
Daily wisdom through quotes and AI-generated art.

Substack : Sneaking Wisdom
Weekly rant and random thoughts.

Cowards

please
 say it
we all feel it
we feel it all

in the air.

muted you are
you said it
we all heard it
we heard it all

the muffle of
your heart
screaming.

If 6 Was 9 to 5

If the sun refused to shine
I don't mind.

The clock keeps on ticking,
Another day goes by
In this mundane routine
I can't help but sigh

My soul chocked,
My mind numb
Trapped in the rat race,
My life undone

I dream of a day,
When I'll be free
To break these chains.

I've got my own life to live
I'm the one who'll have to die
My final task.

So let me live my life
The way I want to

Go ahead on Mr. Businessman
Let it be, it ain't me

make no mistake

you will

   despite hope
   despite love
   despite joy
   despite faith
   leave life

but

you should

   despite fear
   despite pain
   despite them
   despite you
   live life

   for hope
   for love
   for joy
   for faith
   for fear

for pain
for them
for you
for life

Blessedly Cursed

In the ring of our soul
In this cage of us all

We spar with death
All consuming shadow
All alone, yet altogether
Each strike, a bell toll

Death dances
as we grapple
with fate's cruel chime

We give it a good fight
But Death... always victor
Delivering the final blow

But in this fight,
we must give it all
Fear is a fuel
The only one for life

A warrior's last dance.
A warrior's farewell.
Blessedly cursed.

Joy

If
  GOD IS DEAD
  LOVE IS DEAD
  Then why for the love of god
  does it feel so good ?

The key

Discomfort
 Pain
 Fear
 Hatred
 Sadness
 Embarrassment
 Boredom
 Resentment
 Despair

Are open doors
Not sitting rooms

Saints & Sinners

In this sterilized world, we deny our sin,
  They label desires as the darkness within,
  But I'll tell you something, my friend, so true,
  On that original sin, we all carry, me and you.

  The carnal abyss is Plato's cave, you see,
  A choice to be human, to be wild and free,
  In a world so barren, just shadows on the wall
  We reclaim our nature, stand up straight and
tall.

  For love, they say, is the purest of sin,
  The fire that burns for the world to begin,
  They call us all sinners, from the start to the
end,
  But I say we're humans, our desires, our friends,

  In a world that's focused on love oversight,
  To suffocate passion, to deny our delight,
  Set ourselves free for a second we might,
  And in that moment, reclaim our birthright.

Blinded by

Her surprised look
Her annoyed look
Her happy look
Her embarrassed look
Her cheeky look
Her sad look
Her amused look
Her serious look
Her angry look
Her horny look
Her caring look
Her disappointed look

As long as I'm the one
She looks at

Light-Bringer

In dark places
 I provide a blaze
 Yet nobody sees
 The heavy burden of light
 Closing your eyelids
 Sleep well

I'm watching over you.
I'm within you.

Recovery

me
 them

wonders
not mistakes

sprints
not strolls

wanderlust

my precarious heart
on provisory bodies

purgatory
for the
faithful

no 'only one'

but
am I the only one
who believes in

love ?

My only friend

Showed up drunk on life at my goddamn funeral
Everyone who matters to me was there
On my own for the final
That seemed pretty fair

Reaching for those pearly gates
So close yet so far
I just need a hand

I wish my only mate
Wasn't found at a bar
freshly poured whisky blend

Forever stranger

She's sitting next to me
For hours

so close
yet so far

Her shoulder
Her knee and hand
touching mine
makes us giggle

She falls asleep on my shoulder

Flirtatious ignorance
I feel like I'm flying

This single use love
just like us
Is another passenger
in a plane
towards nowhere

She left me

For her destination

Me, part of the journey
Her, another road not taken

My dearly beloved
Forever stranger

All dunhill from here

Lighting up her cigarets with mine's end
And her sentences with mines' ends.

She's burning my life
from both ends

Inspired diatribe
I, out of breath

Each sentence a scorching spark
Our souls igniting
in a roaring blaze

I, rising from her ashes
as
she
flies
away.

Lilith

In stilettos she struts,
 City streets as her runway,
 Sultry confidence.

Each step, a symphony,
Heels click, hearts quicken,
Desire in her wake.

Temptress in red,
Her curves spellbind the night,
My heart skips a beat.

Lipstick and lace,
High heels, her weapon of choice,
She conquers the dark.

A femme fatale's dance,
Until dawn, she owns the night.
And my downfall.

Ø

nobody
 deserves
 it

 good
 or
 bad

 heaven
 of
 hell

 all
 or
 nothing

I want it all

Blue Bird in a Purple Haze

Seeing life through this glass-too-many,
The world's a blur, a hazy dream.
My thoughts are dulled and unsteady,
Drowning in this drunken stream.

Yet in this maze, I find a truth,
A world unseen, where meaning blooms.
For in this state of altered view,
The world reveals some hidden rooms.

Misfits retreat

Through whiskey-soaked nights and neon lights,
Through broken hearts and shattered dreams,

Mocking this decorum we abhor,
In this tangled web of lust and more,

We navigate a riotous sea,
Surfing waves of chaos,
Us, lost boys in Neverland

Shipwrecked or Casted away ?

27

No light
without darkness

No victory
without a fight

Only in the pain
Only in the struggles
Only in the darkness

Can you find
The casted light
Of your mid-crisis life

' LIE '

(NEXT)
 TO
 ME,
 IT
 HURTS
 LESS
 WHEN
 YOU
 LOVE

Faith

with patience as our guide,
to stillness, we'll abide,
so life can provide.

trust the future, open wide,

the current gentle, by my side.

or go against the tide,
up to you to decide.

Mates

Staring at the night sky,
In my life
Not a passer by

Chat by the fire,
Laughters never tire,

Through highs and through lows,
With my friends we compose,
Stories only we know.

Friendship, like old records, plays,
Life's memoirs.

9 789358 737905